MW01681349

Under Purple Skies

- YOU MATTER -

PETER MOLYNEUX

Copyright © 2024 Peter Molyneux
All rights reserved.

ISBN 978-91-987222-1-5

Text © Peter Molyneux 2021
Illustrations © Lailamon 2020

To the reader

First, I want to say thank you for reading this book. I wrote it with you in mind. I hope each story will mean something special to you and to anybody listening.

The book is great for reading independently, for bedtime stories and for group readings.

The nine stories are only subtly connected to each other and can be read on their own, out of context. You might want to limit yourself to one story at a time to leave room for thoughts and conversations.

Now set off for the world with purple skies. I hope you have a good trip.

P.S. There is more information on
www.underpurpleskies.com

Dedicated to Dad,
for inspiration and love.

Contents

Hinkrik

Story 1

Bucky the Bucket Bearer

In a world not so similar to this, yet not entirely different, lived the Bucket Bearers. The Bucket Bearers were beautiful purple creatures on a planet mainly consisting of desert and sea.

Bucky was just three days old. That wasn't so young for a Bucket Bearer; he was already in his late teens. Bucket Bearers only lived for ten days. Like everyone else, he was just over half a meter tall, wore no clothes, had no hair, and had purple skin. The strangest thing about them wasn't their small beady eyes or their long black nails. It wasn't even the glowing cones on their heads. No, the strangest thing about the Bucket Bearers was that almost their entire body looked like a large bucket!

The Bucket Bearers loved to collect water in their buckets. They continuously compared themselves with their friends to see who had the most. But, annoyingly, all the buckets had small holes here and there, from which the water leaked out.

On this particular day, Bucky was sad. He had less water than several of his friends. He was sure he had more holes than the others, and the holes were probably bigger too. Oh, how he hated his holes! Some others had found ways to plug their holes, and some had even managed to build on an extra edge to their buckets so they could hold even more water.

The next day, Bucky came up with an idea. He dug a hole, squeezed himself into it, and the sand around him prevented the water from leaking out. He was quite happy with himself. The entire fourth day and part of the fifth, he sat there ... He was happy ... but not fully happy. Something felt wrong. He tried to be proud of how much water he had, but the thoughts couldn't be kept away.

Is it really meant to be like this, he thought? Everyone tries to collect as much water as they can, but we're all dead after ten days. So, what difference does it make how much water we have?

As he sat there thinking, a friend came by.

"Hi Bucky," he said. "How tragic about your mother."

"Yes, she died yesterday," Bucky replied. "It's a bit sad, but her ten days had passed."

"No, no," the friend replied. "That's not what was tragic; everyone dies. The truly sad thing was that she had almost no water left. Her bucket was completely empty. What a failure and what a wasted life."

Then the friend left. Now Bucky got angry, he stood up and shouted after the friend.

"My mother was not tragic at all! It doesn't matter how much water you have when you die."

Bucky was getting frustrated. He left his hole and set out to find an elderly Bucket Bearer who had known his mother.

"What can I do for you?" He asked as Bucky sat down next to him.

"Was my mother a tragic person? Do you know why she didn't have any water?"

"Come with me," he said and took Bucky to a hill not far away. From there, they had a good view of the surrounding desert.

As Bucky stood there looking, his gaze stuck on a hillside in the distance. On the side of the hill, flowers were growing in the shape of a big heart.

"That's beautiful," Bucky said. "Mom always used to draw little hearts in the sand. How come the flowers are growing in such a beautiful shape?"

"The thing is," his friend said. "That big heart of flowers is something your mother made during her last few days. She was anything but tragic. She left behind something beautiful because she had realized what many fail to understand."

"What do you mean?" Bucky asked.

"This entire world," he continued. "Was created by someone. Even us Bucket Bearers are created and there is a beautiful thought behind each of us. Unfortunately, we are so busy with ourselves that we can spend our entire lives only collecting water. We forget that there is a beautiful reason to our lives."

"What?" asked Bucky. "What's that reason? Tell me!"

"Isn't it obvious?" he said. "Look at yourself … Bucky. You're a Bucket Bearer! Wherever you go, you spread water. Wherever you go, you make plants around you grow. Even the desert blooms when you've been there. Long after your ten days have passed, this world will be beautiful because you were here."

Tears filled Bucky's tiny eyes. He remembered his first morning when he happily jumped and spun around. Laughing and giggling as the water had splashed around him like a sprinkler. Later that very day, he had been told to move carefully and try to cover his holes. How I have wasted my days, he thought. I've been so sad about my leaking water, and it turns out that my holes are the greatest thing I have.

He straightened his back, wiped his eyes and looked up at his new friend. "Tomorrow, I'm not going to save any water," he said. "I will dance, spin and run as far as my short legs can carry me! I'm a Bucket Bearer! My water will make the desert bloom!"

Bucky turned homeward with something new in his eyes. For the first time, he was truly happy. He was proud to be a Bucket Bearer - Bucky the Bucket Bearer.

Hinkrik
Bubblis

Story 2

Angry Bubbly

The story of Bubbly is a bit of a sad story. It took place in the middle of an endless ocean. It was a very peaceful place with crystal clear water as far as the eye could see. And there, in the middle of the sea, was a single, gigantic boat. It had at least twenty floors and was the home of thousands of various creatures. The creatures spent their whole lives on this big boat and were very happy there.

One of these creatures was Bubbly; he was a cute character with big ears and sad eyes. Just under his eyes, he had a trunk that was great for making bubbles. He had a few friends, especially one called Snorkel. Bubbly and Snorkel had been best friends for as long as they could remember, and they always had fun things to do together.

This may not sound like a sad story, but it is. Bubbly made beautiful bubbles, but they also annoyed him because he couldn't really control them. The bubbles just came, especially when he laughed or got angry or tried to scream, then the bubbles just poured out.

One day Bubbly and Snorkel were playing and joking with their other friends. Bubbly started laughing, and when he laughed, lots of bubbles poured out of his trunk.

All his friends thought this was great fun and laughed even more, and so did Bubbly. But soon, Bubbly noticed how he couldn't laugh along. It wasn't funny anymore.

Why are the others laughing? He thought. Do they think I am silly for not being able to control my bubbles?

He wanted them to stop laughing, but they kept on. One of the friends joked about that the captain had brought Bubbly on this trip so everyone would have something to laugh at. Now Bubbly got angry, and when Bubbly got angry, even more bubbles poured out. The friends couldn't stop themselves from roaring with laughter. He tried to shout "STOP!" but more bubbles just came out of his trunk. Even his best friend Snorkel was laughing. No one seemed to care. Unable to scream,

he waved his trunk around in the hope of slapping someone so they would understand. But they didn't seem to care. They just pushed Bubbly away and kept laughing. Bubbly was so angry he wanted to explode. Why couldn't anyone see that he was sad!

In the end, tears began to run down his face. He didn't want the others to notice, so he tried to run away. But there were so many bubbles everywhere that he ran straight into a wall and collapsed on the slippery floor. He was lying there on his back with bubbles everywhere and his friends' laughter echoing in his head. He just wanted to close his eyes and cover his ears, sink through the floor, and disappear. Eventually, he managed to crawl out of the room.

Angry and hurt, Bubbly searched for a place where the others wouldn't find him. He found a hidden stairway and made his way down as far as he could ... until he got to the bottom of the big boat. There, behind a metal door, he found a small room that no one seemed to use. The room was dark and quiet; it felt good. But he was still furious. He hated his silly trunk, and he hated all his so-called friends. He hated this boat, and he hated the captain who had invited him on this trip.

Several days later, when Bubbly was still sitting in his room at the bottom of the boat, somebody slowly opened the door. It was Snorkel! Snorkel had finally found where he was hiding. Bubbly wasn't happy to see him at all.

Who did Snorkel think he was? No real friend would have laughed at Bubbly like Snorkel did, and no real friend would have let him sit here alone for several days.

Before Snorkel even had time to say hello, Bubbly found a broom and threw it, so it hit Snorkel right in the face. Then he ran to the door.

"Get out!" he shouted. "Go back to your new friends. I never want to see you again." He slammed the door as hard as he could.

Now he was alone again, and Snorkel probably wouldn't come back. Bubbly wanted Snorkel to be sad. He even hoped it had hurt when the broom hit his face. He curled up in the corner again. He felt like the loneliest person in the world. No one likes me, he thought. And that's ok because I don't like them either.

Bubbly became angrier with each passing day. He never wanted to see anyone again. There, in the dark, bad thoughts started to grow. He wanted revenge. He wanted to destroy. He wanted to find something sharp

Bubbly
Angry

and make holes in the bottom of the boat. He wanted to ruin everything.

What Bubbly didn't know was that Snorkel was on the other side of the door. Snorkel had been there several times but had not dared to go back inside. This whole situation had made Snorkel so sad. What had happened to his friend? If he could just go in and talk to him. Then he would understand that Snorkel was sorry and that he missed him. He heard Bubbly hitting the floor with something hard in there. It didn't sound like this was a good time. Maybe tomorrow, Snorkel thought. Maybe he won't be as angry tomorrow.

Hinkrik
Goffarna

Story 3

The War of the Goffs

The Goffs lived underground, in a world of caves. They looked like hairy lumps, had big eyes, a big mouth and two small feet, and that's about it. Oh yes, they also had a long saggy nose hanging out from the middle of their face. The Goffs loved hard work, chewing their way through soil and dirt to create passageways and caves. The goal was to enlarge their underground realm.

Unfortunately, they hardly got anywhere with it. You see, there were two kinds of Goffs, and they were enemies. One kind, called Shaggy-Goffs, had hair all over the place. The other kind were called Silk-Goffs, and they had straight pink hair. They had been at war for as long as anyone could remember. They didn't have weapons but fought to destroy each other's caves. This never-ending war meant that they didn't have much time to work on extending their own kingdom.

Among the Shaggy-Goffs, there was a happy little guy named Mini-Goff. He wanted to start working like everyone else but was told that he was too small. Mini-Goff got very frustrated when he heard that. He wasn't small at all. He had even stopped sucking on his nose. (Goffs suck on their noses when they are small because they do not have a thumb).

Mini-Goff didn't just want to watch. He started digging a little when no one could see him. One day he accidentally dug too far, creating a hole in a wall. The hole went right into a cave that belonged to the enemies, the Silk-Goffs. There in the middle of the room, sat a small figure who was still sucking on her nose. Her name was Pink. Mini-Goff looked at her and wondered how such a cute Goff could be an enemy.

She looked just like a regular Shaggy-Goff, but with slightly different hair. She definitely didn't look angry or dangerous. Mini-Goff stood there for a while, looking and thinking. Why are our people fighting? Imagine how much we could accomplish if we didn't ruin things for each other. This war thing ... feels so silly.

"Why are we enemies?" he asked suddenly. Pink quickly looked around and discovered the hole in the wall where Mini-Goff stood. She became nervous and sucked her nose even harder.

Mini-Goff smiled and said: "Do you still suck your nose?" Pink quickly spat out her nose. It flew up and slapped her on the forehead and then flopped from cheek to cheek.

Her nose was still wet, but she tried to look grown-up. "No," she answered. "Don't be ridiculous. I'm not a baby!"

Mini-Goff burst into laughter, and so did Pink. From that day on, they were best friends. Every day they played together secretly when no one could see them. But there was no good place to play, and they longed to build and dig.

One day, Mini-Goff had an idea. Above the ground, no one ever worked. They could build things up there without being discovered. Pink and Mini-Goff were excited to give this crazy idea a try. When most others were working, and nobody noticed, they would sneak up above ground.

Together they began to create something that had never been done before. First, Mini-Goff and Pink started by digging out a big hole. Then, they dug a channel to the sea so that water could flow in and fill the hole. The result was the world's first swimming pool.

They were almost done when Pink's big brother suddenly stood right next to them.

"What is this?" he asked without wanting an answer. "I knew you were doing something forbidden. I will report this!" He quickly ran back down under the ground.

Pink was terrified. "We have to hide," she said. "They're going to put us in jail."

"No," Mini-Goff replied calmly. "If they think the pool looks fun, maybe they won't be angry. Hurry! Let's get this finished."

They built a long slide with all the soil they dug up from the hole. It ended with a jump. It was super cool! You could get up to a remarkable speed, shooting through the air before landing in the middle of the pool.

They had only had time to try the slide once before Pink's brother came back, and this time with a group of Silk-Goff teenagers. At the same time, a group of

Shaggy-Goff teenagers had pitched up on the other side of the pool. They stood there looking at each other and at the pool. They didn't look happy.

"What's going on here?" one of the Shaggy-Goffs asked. Mini-Goff knew this was a defining moment.

He stood up so everyone could see him. He declared in a loud voice: "This is an adventure land that belongs to all Goffs together. Everyone can play, but if you're here, you have to be nice." Now the teenagers were in a tricky spot. Mini-Goff and Pink really deserved to be punished and the pool destroyed. But at the same time, they had never tried a slide and pool before.

As they stood there trying to decide what to do, a couple of teenagers couldn't resist any longer and ran for the slide. They literally screamed with joy as they swooped down the slide and shot through the air.

After that, no one could hold back. Within seconds, everyone was playing. It was the first time ever that Shaggy-Goffs and Silky-Goffs had had fun together.

Every day they played together, and every day they added more things to the cool adventure park. More and more Goffs came to play and help. At first, only the young ones, but soon the older Goffs also started to

join. In the end, everyone was there, and the war thing became something of the past.

Now they worked together and didn't destroy each other's caves. They could finally extend their kingdoms fast.

Mini-Goff and Pink became the heroes of the century. Ending a long war and starting a new era of play, friendship, and cooperation.

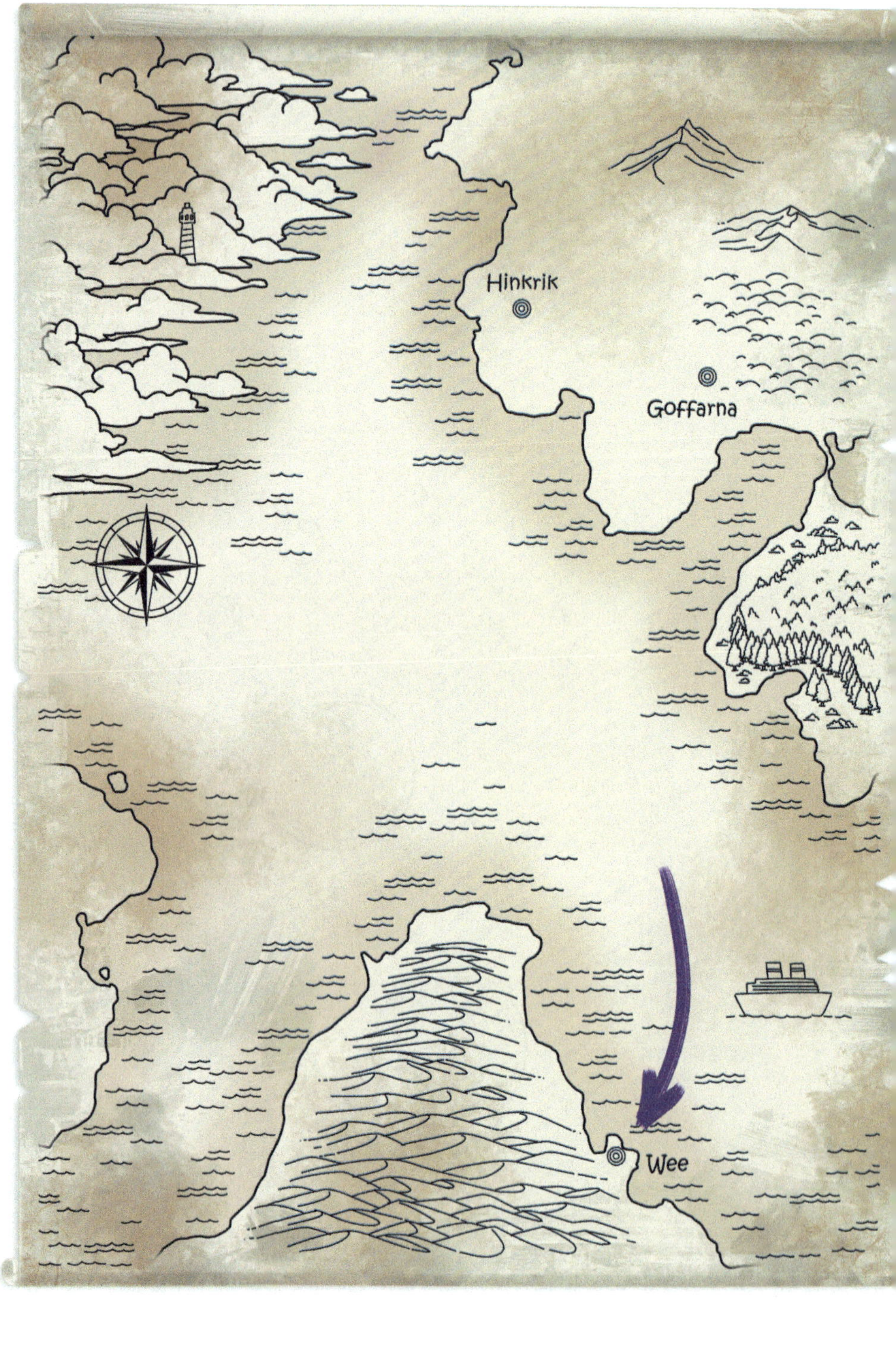
Hinkrik
Goffarna
Wee

Story 4

The Letter to Wee

Wee found himself standing on an empty beach. He couldn't remember how long he'd been standing there or how he got there. Maybe he'd always been there. But it was an excellent place to stand. There was nothing wrong with it at all. The sky above him was purple and peaceful.

In Wee's world, there was almost nothing, just sand, sand, and more sand. There were no plants, no animals, no mountains and not so much as a pebble. Where the sand ended, a seemingly infinite sea began that was perfectly still and beautiful.

Suddenly he noticed something unusual happening way out on the horizon. Wee couldn't remember anything ever happening before. But now, something was definitely happening. Something was

approaching... It was a big boat, and it got closer and closer as if it were aiming for Wee. When it was near, it stopped, and a small empty rowing boat was released. It came straight at him and stopped as it reached the sand in front of Wee's feet.

Wee stood there for a while, looking at the big boat and then at the small boat. He couldn't quite grasp what was going on and what he should do next. He tried to think. The first thought that came to mind was: wow, but then he couldn't think of anything else, so he stopped thinking. In the middle of the small boat was a white envelope. This made Wee curious. He reached down and picked it up. On it were the words: "To Wee".

To me! That's nice, Wee thought and started opening the envelope. It took some time: opening envelopes was apparently not Wee's thing. His fingers were way too short and thick. Eventually, he tore into it and found a small note inside. It said:

Hi Wee, take a seat in the boat. This is where your journey begins.

A smile spread across Wee's face. There was something special about this moment. He had been standing on this beach all his life. Now he felt this might be what he had been waiting for. Finally, he thought. This is where my journey begins.

Wee sat down in the small rowing boat, and it took him to the big ship. Onboard, he entered a dark corridor. Hearing distant voices, laughter, and music, Wee felt nervous. He started walking, and soon he found himself in a big hall. There were people everywhere, some dancing, some laughing.

Wow! Wee had never seen anything like it. From the ceiling hung large chandeliers and lianas that some were swinging from. Wee stood there staring for ages. Everything was so fantastic, and Wee drooled without even noticing.

"Are you new here?" somebody asked. Somebody had come right up close to Wee and beamed at him with a big smile. He was light blue with a trunk, big eyes and big floppy ears. "My name is Snorkel," he added.

"Hi," Wee said, wiping his mouth. "Yes, I'm new here. My name is Wee"

"Oh," Snorkel said. "Can I show you around?"

This was the beginning of a long friendship. And the big hall was just the first of all the things he was about to discover. Together they played in the water park, went to the movies, bowling and go-karting, sang karaoke, played football, ate ice cream and sweets, swung on the giant swings, and built huts in the trees (because there were beautiful trees growing inside the boat). The fun never ended. There was even a giant ball pit and large pillow rooms. One of Snorkel's favorites was the arcade, where there were lots of awesome video games.

Everybody on the boat seemed to have the same goal: to fill every day with as much fun as possible.

One day they took a break from all the fun and stood up on deck looking out to sea.

"I love this boat," Wee said with his eyes fixed on the horizon.

"Me too," Snorkel replied. "Do you remember your first day here? You were so amazed by everything that you were drooling. I immediately thought this guy just has to be new here."

"Yes, I remember," Wee replied. "It must be a couple of years ago now. How time flies."

They stood there together in silence, looking out over the water. Wee broke the silence again.

"Snorkel ... you once told me that you were also picked up by a small rowing boat while standing on a beach."

"That's right," Snorkel replied. "And there was a letter in the boat with my name on it."

"Yes," Wee said. "That's exactly how it was. Now there is a question that keeps coming back to me. Maybe it sounds silly, but this is it: Who wrote the letter?" He looked at Snorkel and then at the horizon before continuing: "Someone must have written it, and that someone knew your name. Isn't it strange? What if it's the same person who built this boat. Could that person know where we are heading?"

"Wow, those are big questions," Snorkel replied. "Actually, none of that has ever crossed my mind. If you knew who it was ... what would you do?"

Wee had to think a bit and then said: "I think I'd just want to say thank you, for all this. And I'd ask a lot of questions, like, 'Where are we going?' ... and 'What is the best thing you can do on this boat'. Wouldn't you like that, Snorkel?" Snorkel was too slow to answer, so Wee continued.

"What if the person who built this boat is here somewhere ... Imagine, Snorkel, if you could make this trip with the one who invited us. That would be so awesome. I'm sure the one who saw me on the beach and knew my name, sees me now too. I think that person is glad you and I became friends, Snorkel."

"Yes," Snorkel said. "Actually, I think so, too. And you know, Wee? I'd say thank you for Wee, because you're the best thing on this whole boat."

Wee was so happy he gave Snorkel a hug ... or tried anyway; his arms could not reach around Snorkel. Skipping the hug, they stood there in silence, looking out to sea. They stood there thinking about that strange question:

Who wrote the letter?

Jackie
Hinkrik
Goffarna
Wee

Story 5

Wild Jackie on the Clouds

The journey began with Jackie and everyone else boarding the cloud ship. It was a giant flying city, made entirely of fluffy, cloud-like, material. They boarded by walking up a long flight of stairs. On the way up, a large hairy figure stood and handed out jackets to them. They were very nice jackets and everyone got their own.

Just as Jackie had boarded the ship and got her jacket on, she tripped and fell, face down, to the ground. The ground was like a soft pillow. It didn't hurt at all; in fact, it was lovely. It was so bouncy that Jackie bounced right back to her feet. This was cool. She quickly looked around. Even the houses were built of fluffy cloud-like material. Jackie had an idea, and just had to try it out. She ran as fast as she could, straight into the wall of a house. It was soft, squishy, and so bouncy that she was thrown back into the air. She landed on her feet, meters away from the house. Wow, this was amazing. It felt like the best place in the whole universe. Jackie must have looked crazy because she ran and threw herself at everything she could see. No wonder they called her Wild Jackie.

The trip took many years. Sometimes it got freezing cold. It could even snow. Fortunately, they had their jackets. The jackets kept you warm no matter how cold it was. They also kept you cool no matter how hot it was. They protected against rain and wind and never seemed to wear out.

Jackie liked the snow, but the rain was even better. When the clouds were wet, you could run and slide several hundred meters. A lot of people liked to play like that, but not Shy Boo. Shy Boo was a little nervous and careful. The others avoided him when they were going to run over to the big hill to play.

One day when it had rained, Jackie decided to make a world record at sliding. She ran as fast as she could, threw herself on her stomach and slid at super high speed. What she didn't know was that someone else had had the same idea but from the opposite direction. Unable to turn, the two slid straight into each other with

a bang. This wasn't good. They hit each other so hard that Jackie passed out for a few minutes.

Jackie was in pain, but she was glad to still be alive. For days she felt so battered and bruised that she couldn't jump and play as usual. Instead, Jackie started thinking about her jacket. Why was she wearing a jacket? She had always taken it for granted, but now she started to think about how amazing it really was.

She stopped a friend and asked: "Isn't it amazing that we have such good jackets?"

"What do you mean?" the friend answered. "Everyone wears jackets like this, what else would we wear?"

"But you don't get it," Jackie said. "What if our jackets weren't water resistant or broke easily. What if we didn't have jackets, we'd have frozen to death!"

Her friend walked away because she thought Jackie was talking nonsense. But Jackie kept thinking. This was a jacket mystery, and it needed to be solved. For days, she tried to figure out what kind of jacket it was. No one could help. Eventually, she started to look for clues inside the jacket. There on the inside, at the back of her neck, she found a small label. The label had the brand

Staggelini printed on it. Jackie picked up her phone and started searching for information about Staggelini. When she found it, she almost passed out again. The jacket she was wearing was worth ten million dollars. It was unbelievable. Jackie just had to shout it out:

"It's worth ten million dollars!"

She stopped a couple more friends.

"Our jackets are Staggelini! They're worth ten million dollars!" But her friends laughed at her.

Everyone was heading over to the big hill to slide and bounce. Jackie wanted to join them, but she was still in too much pain. She looked around and saw that Shy Boo was the only one left. He was sitting on his own with his knees pulled up.

When Jackie limped up to him, she heard Shy Boo sobbing.

"Are you crying?" she asked.

"Yes," Shy Boo replied. "Nobody cares about me. Nobody wants me to play. Nobody wants to be my friend. I'm totally worthless."

Jackie sat quietly for a while before saying:

“Let me tell you something Shy Boo. The guy who gave you your jacket, he cares about you. You know what that jacket cost? Because I happen to know. It's a Staggelini and it's worth ten million dollars.”

Shy Boo looked up with big eyes.

“The guy who gave me the jacket thinks I'm worth ten million dollars! There's someone who cares about me!” Shy Boo smiled so much that it looked like he was going to crack.

“In fact, there are two people who care about you,” Jackie continued. “I like you too. There's a little hill over there where we can bounce and play without it being frightening. Do you want to go there with me now?”

“I'd love to,” Shy Boo answered.

Then they held hands, and Limping Jackie and Happy Boo went off to play.

Jackie
Hinkrik
Goffarna
Kaptenen
Wee

Story 6

The Captain

In a world of purple skies, large moons, and an almost infinitely calm sea lived Snorkel and Wee. They lived on a giant boat in the middle of the great sea. It was a wonderful boat with everything you could wish for. Together, they had recently started to ask themselves questions about life on the boat. For example, who wrote the letter inviting them on this journey, who was steering the boat, and where they were heading? Wee, who was the big thinker of the two, suggested one day that they should go and see if they could find a captain on the boat.

"There's got to be a captain somewhere," Wee said. "If he is here, we can find him."

“Yes,” Snorkel replied. “I think that sounds like an epic adventure! We've been almost everywhere; nobody knows this boat better than we do.”

“But I would guess,” said Wee. “That you can go both further down and further up than we have ever been.” Snorkel suddenly got very excited. His eyes shot up as he slapped Wee with his trunk ...

“Why didn’t I think about this before,” he said, “I know where there's a secret stairway.” He eagerly continued to talk: “Next to the big cinema where Trumpet usually sits. There's a hidden door, that leads to a stairway.”

Wee also got excited. “Perfect, we'll go there right now,” he said.

“No, no,” Snorkel interrupted. “We have to wait so no one sees us.”

The following morning, before anyone had woken up, they sneaked away to the big cinema. They found the hidden door, though it was small and barely visible. Right in front of the door lay Trumpet, and she was sleeping. Trumpet was a small, cute figure with a head shaped like a trumpet.

She was timid and never spoke to anyone. They grabbed Trumpet's feet and pulled her aside. She woke up a little bit, mumbled something strange and fell asleep again.

Snorkel and Wee gently pushed the door open, and inside there was, indeed, a secret stairway. Wee only had to glance at the long staircase, and he had made up his mind.

"It's much easier to go down than to go up," he said, starting to run down the stairs. Snorkel ran behind with his short thick legs while shouting:

"There's no point! I already know what's at the bottom."

But Wee didn't listen. He kept running until he reached the bottom. He found himself in front of a steel door. On the door was a small sign that read:

You're not wanted here! Go away!

Snorkel was out of breath when he came down but managed to gasp: "Don't go in there, there's someone in there who's very angry." Wee looked at him anxiously.

"But what else can we do?" he asked. "There aren't any other doors."

"We'll have to go back up, but I'm already tired, and it's pretty far if we're going to the top."

"We have to try," Wee said, starting to walk. The first floors were relatively easy, but then it got harder. Step by step, they walked up and with each step they got a little slower. Snorkel was exhausted. His legs were definitely not made to be used. When Snorkel got too tired, Wee tried to help by pushing him. In the end, they just couldn't take another step. Snorkel sat down, and Wee sat next to him.

"I can't make it any further!" Snorkel moaned, almost bursting into tears. "I wish the captain could help us." Snorkel had barely had time to say this before they heard footsteps.

As they looked up the stairs, they saw the two big feet of a soft, white furry creature.

Wee and Snorkel had never seen anyone that huge before. Thick legs, arms and fingers, a big hairy face, and black beady eyes ... With a pleasantly calm and soft voice, he said:

"Are you on your way up? You look tired, do you want me to carry you?" Wee shone up:

"Would you really? That would be so nice."

Instantly they sat in his furry arms as he took giant steps up the stairs.

It was so warm and comfy in his arms. It felt like they never wanted to be put down. But the journey ended almost before it started.

“We’re at the top now,” The captain said. “This is my control tower.” He carefully put them down. Wee and Snorkel looked around with big eyes. It was absolutely magical. There was floor to ceiling windows in every direction, with a beautiful view of the sea, the horizon and the purple sky. There were also lots of screens, buttons, levers and dials that looked very cool but were utterly impossible to understand.

Snorkel stood for a long time, looking at the buttons and screens. Then suddenly, Snorkel asked the captain:

“Who are you?”

“I have many names,” he answered. “But I think it’s best if you just call me Captain.”

“Wow that's good,” Snorkel said. “Then we've succeeded with our mission.”

Wee was not as interested in all the buttons. Instead, he stood staring out over the beautiful sea. He barely heard what the others were talking about because his thoughts were far away.

"The letter," he suddenly said. He looked at the captain and asked, "Did you write the letter?"

The captain was silent for a moment while he looked at Wee with kind eyes. "Yes, I wrote the letter." Wee continued with more questions: "But how did you know my name? How did you know I was there? Why did you want me on the boat?"

"My child," he said calmly. "Of course, I wanted you here on the boat, where else would I want you to be? You see, a long, long time ago, a tear fell from my eye, I caught it and it turned into a beautiful pearl in my hand. I looked at it and knew that no matter how beautiful I thought it was, it needed to be in a different place to come to life. I found a good beach and before I buried it, I named it Wee."

This wasn't easy for Wee to understand. Still, he listened carefully as the captain continued: "I left you there in the sand so that you could grow. My eyes saw you all the time. Every second I longed for you. But one day the time had finally come. I steered the boat across the seas with my sight set on the beach where you were standing."

His smile grew a little as he continued: "You could never imagine how happy I was when you boarded the boat. I'm so glad you love life here and that you've found a friend in Snorkel."

Wee stood there, amazed, looking at the captain. Tears filled his big eyes. He didn't know why the tears were coming, but he knew that he had never felt this way before.

It felt like all the fun he had had on this boat wasn't worth anything compared to standing right here, right now, hearing that he had been longed for and loved every single day …

The captain turned to Snorkel.

"Snorkel, where's your friend?" he asked.

"What do you mean?" Snorkel replied. "Wee is right here."

The captain looked a bit serious. "Your other friend, the friend who's alone right now, the friend who needs you?"

Snorkel understood that it was Bubbly the captain was referring to. He felt so ashamed that he looked down at his feet.

"No, you don't have to look away," the captain continued in the same friendly voice. "I don't want you to be ashamed. I want you to understand. You probably heard what I was telling Wee, and you probably understand how much I love him.

The same goes for you Snorkel; I love you in the same way. I longed for you just as much when you were standing on your beach. But I want you to understand; I love Bubbly in exactly the same way too. You're all so incredibly precious to me. Please, take care of each other."

The three of them stood silent for a while, and then the captain continued: "My children, now you've got something to think about. Go back now, continue to enjoy life on this boat and I hope to see you again soon." The two friends said thank you and went back down the stairs.

They had met the captain. What a day! Would life ever be the same again?

Hinkrik
Jackie
Goffarna
Morpho
Wee

Story 7

Morpho, Defender of the Galaxy

High up among the thin clouds, Morpho and his ship were slowly floating through the purple sky. If you had asked Morpho, he would have said he was the one and only Defender of the Galaxy, a respected hero. But the reality was something entirely different. Morpho looked a lot like a centipede. A centipede has legs along his entire body, but not Morpho. Instead he had a long line of hands.

It would have been much better if Morpho had had legs because then he could have walked. With fingers, he could only scratch his way forward in a very clumsy way. There was one detail that made

Morpho the clumsiest creature ever. A tall and wide plate stood straight up from his back, almost like on a dinosaur. The plate, which was bright yellow and larger than Morphos' entire body, was very clumsy but also perfect for air surfing. But more about air surfing in a minute.

If an enemy appeared, Morpho would shoot them down with laser cannons before they even knew he'd seen them. No one messes with the Defender of the Galaxy! That was what Morpho thought, but the reality was, of course, quite different. In fact, Morpho had never been able to defend anyone against anything. Morpho's ship had no laser cannons; it didn't have any weapons at all. His ship couldn't even be steered because ... The fact of the matter is that ... the ship was nothing more than a large shiny bubble. Morpho was helplessly drifting around in ... a bubble.

Sometimes Morpho was worried that his bubble would burst. Without a bubble, he would go free-falling towards the ocean way below. A fall towards death. In fact, it had happened several times. He wouldn't have been so lucky if it hadn't been for the big yellow plate on his back. Morpho could use it to

surf through the air. Air surfing was a lot of fun, but it was a dangerous game. As soon as possible, he would have to find a new bubble and dive into it. So far, he had always succeeded because there used to be a lot of bubbles to dive into. But Morpho was worried now because lately, he hadn't seen any other bubbles. So right now, he really didn't want his bubble to burst.

One day, as Morpho sat there enjoying yet another beautiful sunrise, he sensed something in the corner of his eye. He turned around as fast as he could, ready to use his laser cannons.

It wasn't an enemy; it just turned out to be another bubble. But there was someone in it, someone with a big yellow plate on her back.

The figure in the second bubble looked exactly like Morpho. She looked like a twin. Morpho got annoyed. Who did the other one think she was? "I'm the Defender of the Galaxy," he said. Don't come here and think you're important. This is my heaven, my galaxy. Get out of my way!"

If they had engines, they could have left each other. Now, they just had to wait for the wind to help them.

But the wind was not on anyone's side. Slowly they floated closer and closer together until, finally, the bubbles were pressed against each other. It was as if fate was mocking them. With more space than anybody could ask for and not another bubble in sight, the pair were pressed against each other, slowly drifting through the thin air.

So it went on for days. As time passed, something started to happen to Morpho. The irritation slowly disappeared. Morpho began to relax and enjoy letting his gaze disappear into her eye. Her eye was more mystical and beautiful than the sky around him. He named her Yellow after her beautiful yellow plate. Soon he realized that it felt pretty good to have Yellow so close.

Even the most beautiful sunsets were forgotten because Morpho simply didn't want to look at anything but Yellow. He kind of forgot that he wanted to be the Defender of the Galaxy.

Weeks passed, and the pair floated slowly through the endless, quiet purple sky. They were like a romantic couple who couldn't imagine life apart. But suddenly, a gust of wind came along and caused the bubbles to disconnect. The bubbles started floating away from each other.

Morpho had never felt such a panic in his life. "No, no please stay!" he shouted out. Morpho could see how sad Yellow was. He wanted to comfort her, but he was utterly powerless; they both were.

Slowly, they floated away, farther and farther apart. Morpho realized now that they would never see each other again.

Suddenly something even worse happened: Yellow's bubble burst, and she quickly began to fall. Morpho saw the terror in her eye. There were no new bubbles. There was nothing but thin air all the way down to the sea surface.

Morpho couldn't save Yellow, but maybe he could hold her hand just for a short while. There was no time to think, so Morpho made a crazy decision, he burst his own bubble.

Now they were both falling, and there was no rescue in sight. But they had one goal: to reach each other. They used their plates to steer closer together. Falling quickly, faster and faster, with the deadly sea surface approaching rapidly. They were so close to each other that their hands could almost reach each other.

Morpho tried to reach for Yellow, but the wind seemed too strong. But suddenly, one of his hands could reach one of hers. Before they knew what was happening, all their hands could grip each other. Their fingers were braided together, and their eyes pressed close together.

They were still falling and had gained such a speed that the wind pushed tears from their eyes. There was no hope, they knew that, but their clinging hands undoubtedly stated: "I will never, ever let you go".

To slow the fall slightly, the two simultaneously tried to push their plates out to the sides. To their great surprise, they completely stopped falling. Their plates moved like wings. They were flying.

Wow! What a feeling! Morpho screamed out: "We're flying! We're flying!" He had had the clumsiest body anybody could imagine, but now they could move freely in any direction they wanted. They could fly high or dive low...they were free.

The world was different. The sea wasn't a danger anymore; it was beautiful. The anxiety and loneliness were gone. Together Morpho and Yellow were something new, something better, something beautiful. They had become Yellow Morpho – A beautiful butterfly, like a flower against the purple sky.

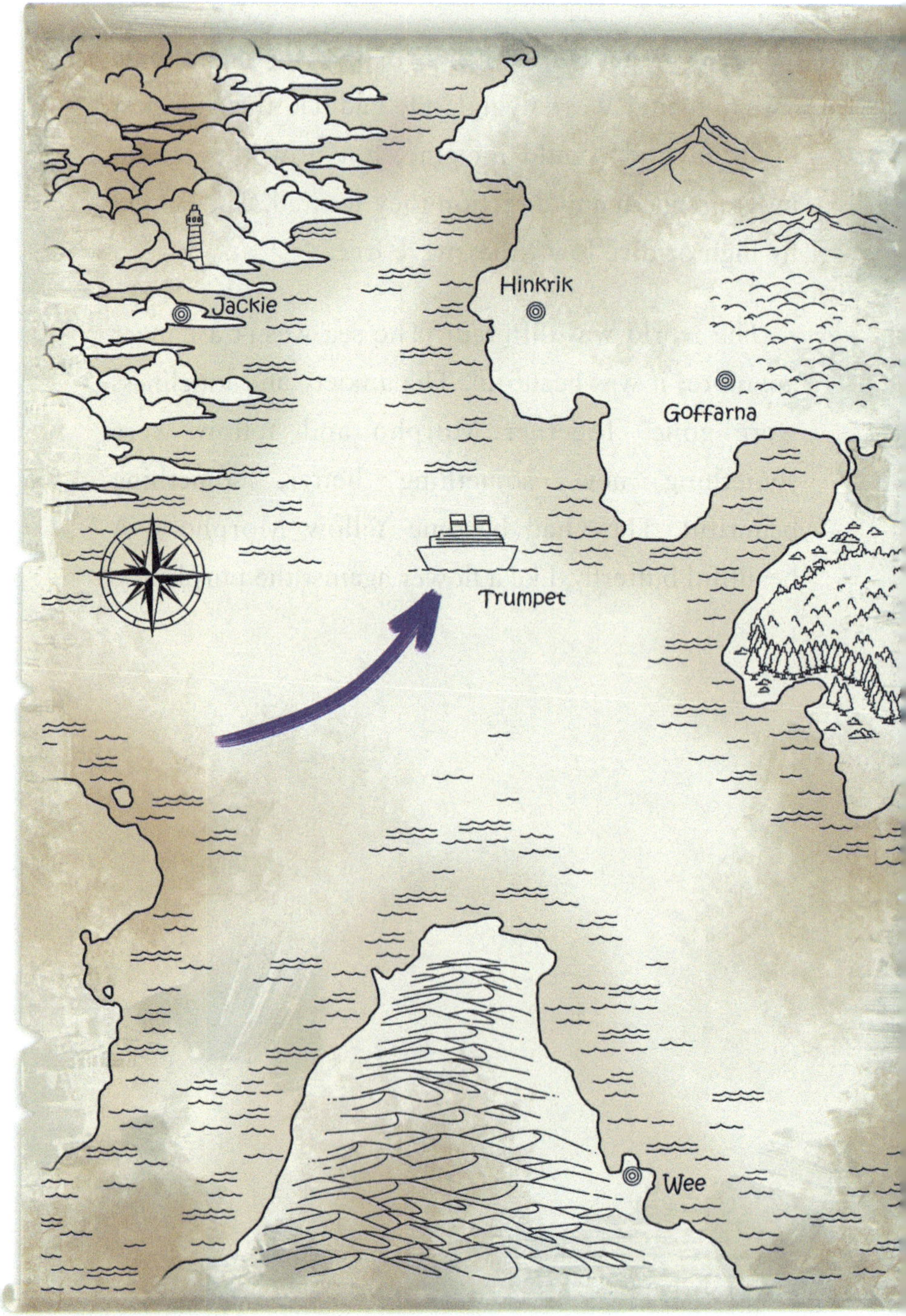
Hinkrik
Jackie
Goffarna
Trumpet
Wee

Story 8

Trumpet Calling

On the big boat in the middle of the sea, there was a very small and shy character called Trumpet. She had a favorite place in a corner outside the cinema. Trumpet looked a little odd. Her feet looked like they belonged to a duck and her head looked like a trumpet. Her body was small and thin; she could rarely be of any use.

She could talk, but her voice was so unclear that no one understood her. That's why Trumpet preferred to be alone. Sometimes, someone would ask something, but Trumpet was usually too shy to answer. If she did, she mumbled in a way that nobody could understand. Most of the time, Trumpet stood with her head pressed against the wall and looked down at her feet to avoid drawing attention. Meeting others and talking was scary. It wasn't that they were mean to her. In fact, everyone Trumpet had met had been kind. But it was still scary, and she was always nervous.

What Trumpet didn't realize was that she was standing with her head pressed against a secret door. She didn't know who was on the other side of that door. But somebody was there, somebody who saw Trumpet despite the wall between them. It was a great furry creature who had built the entire boat. Although he could ask anyone, he would soon ask Trumpet to help with an important task.

One day, Trumpet stood, as usual, with her head pressed against the wall when she suddenly heard a voice speaking.

A calm and pleasant voice said: "Trumpet, dear Trumpet, I need your help. Someone has made holes in the boat and we're sinking. I'm the captain. I want you to tell everyone that the boat is sinking but that there is no need for worry. I have prepared a new country where we will arrive soon. Tell

everyone to get up on deck so they can get off the boat as soon as we arrive. I have a lot of boats to steer, so I need your help with this right now."

The voice stopped talking. Trumpet stood absolutely still. She didn't dare to move an inch. Had she just heard a voice? It must have been a dream or just thoughts inside her own head. It couldn't have been the captain, could it? If so, where did the voice come from? There was definitely no captain around. There were many people outside the cinema, but none as close as the voice had been. Trumpet decided to forget about it.

By the way, she thought. If it had been the captain, he probably would have known that I am NOT the right person for such a task.

No one would listen to what Trumpet said, no one would understand her, and, in fact, no one would even hear that she was trying to say something. The mere thought of speaking in front of everyone made Trumpet completely stiff with fear. She wouldn't be able to make a sound even if she tried. No, she might as well forget about all this.

For several seconds, Trumpet tried to think of something else. It was no use. Had she heard the captain's voice? Where did it come from? Did the captain really want to tell her all this? Was the boat really sinking? The thoughts were spinning, and Trumpet couldn't let them go. She knew why she couldn't ignore the thoughts. It was because this was real. She hadn't imagined it. The captain needed her help, and it was important.

Her whole body trembled. She pressed her head harder against the wall and tried to become invisible. She couldn't tell everyone ... But she wanted to ... No, she didn't want to ... Oh, how difficult everything had become. In the end, she gathered the courage to talk to the captain even though she did not know where he was. The only thing she managed to produce was a faint mumble that no one could understand. What she wanted to say was:

“Captain, help, I'm afraid. What should I do? I can’t even speak so that people understand me.”

The captain apparently understood her mumbling because the captain's calm voice was heard again:

“Trumpet my child, you may not think you're good at anything, but you're just as good as I want you to be. You're not made to talk quietly. You're made to shout out loud. You're Trumpet. No one can shout as loudly and as clearly as you. You've just never dared to try.”

Now Trumpet was sure it was not her imagination. She had heard the voice again. She was still terrified but also encouraged. She began to straighten up and stopped pushing her head against the wall. Could it be true that she was good at something? Could there be a reason why her head looked like a trumpet? She whispered to herself: “I am Trumpet, and no one can shout as loudly and as clearly as I can. The captain needs me, and I can do it.”

Slowly she turned around and looked at everyone standing outside the cinema. She straightened up even more. She took a deep breath, and then ... it happened. She did it! She shouted as loud and clear as she could. Her voice echoed all over the boat in a way no one had heard before.

"This is a message from the captain: The boat is sinking! Get up on deck! A new country awaits!"

What a feeling it was for Trumpet: She had done it, she was brave, she was good! Happy and proud, she whispered again: "I am Trumpet, and no one can shout as loud and clear as I can. The captain needs me, and I can do it".

And then Trumpet shouted out the message over, and over, and over again. It worked, everyone heard her, all over the boat, and everyone listened. They all started moving up towards the deck. What a feeling, what a wonderful feeling. Trumpet followed them up onto the deck. On the way, many people patted her on the back and said: "Well done, Trumpet!"

On the deck, a magnificent sight awaited. The boat was just close to land, on the way into a large bay. The country looked breathtaking, with green rolling hills covered with the most beautiful flowers one could imagine. The big boat was not alone. There were lots of big boats all on their way into the bay at the same time. Some had already reached land, while others were still approaching. And over their heads, large airships flew in. Everyone seemed to have precisely the same goal, and everyone seemed to arrive at the same time.

What was this? What was happening? Trumpet did not know, but she did know one thing: The captain had chosen her for an important task today. A task that no one could have performed as well as her.

Jackie
Hinkrik
Hamnen
Goffarna
Wee

Story 9

The Party in the Harbor

The big boat was about to sink because someone had made holes in it. Fortunately, it reached land before sinking entirely. Everyone stepped ashore. All but one; Bubbly. He made the holes in the boat, and he wanted it to sink. Bubbly would rather sink with it than go ashore with the captain and everybody else. So, he stayed in his little room at the bottom of the boat.

When everyone else had gone ashore, the boat continued to sink until it was immersed underwater. The boat sank slowly through the dark water. With each meter, Bubbly became angrier and angrier. He was angry at all those who had teased him. He was angry at the captain who had brought him on this boat and for giving him a trunk that made bubbles.

The boat sank to the bottom of the sea, and it kept sinking. It continued down through the mud. The mud turned to stone above the boat, so that Bubbly would never, ever be able to get back up. The boat sank through lava and fire and continued sinking. In the end, it landed at the bottom of the darkness. There, in the boat, in darkness, sat an angry, scared, and lonely Bubbly. He hated everything, he hated this place, the captain, and he even hated himself.

Above land, everyone gathered for the big celebration the captain had prepared. It was an opening party for those who had come to the new country. Tables stood in long rows and were so long that you could not even see the ends of them. The tables were set with fine white linen tablecloths, beautiful crystal glasses, and place name cards on each plate. At the front of the stage was a band playing music, and next to them stood the captain. He looked out at the crowd as they began to sit down. He was delighted. The captain had longed for this day. Finally, all his children were gathered. The tables were set, the music was playing, everyone had sat down. Everything was ready, and the party could begin.

But the smile dropped from the captain's face. His eyes were fixed on an empty chair. The plate had a small sign with the name Bubbly written on it. The captain stepped forward. “Stop playing,” he said firmly to the band. You could hear a pin drop as everybody looked at the captain.

“There's not going to be a party,” he said.

Wee ran up to him to calm him down.

“Please, captain, can't you see how many people are here? Don't you see how happy they are and the anticipation? Everyone else is here, there's only one person who didn't want to come.”

The captain almost looked angry, and he answered so that everybody could hear.

“You say that there's only one person who didn't want to come. But I can't be happy; I can't have a party. I have loved Bubbly for a thousand years and now he is far from here, alone, and scared. There won't be a party unless Bubbly is here.”

He walked between the tables with determined and heavy steps toward the small wooden jetty by the sea.

The captain did not hesitate, despite the cold water, but dived straight in. He knew exactly where he was going. There was no time to lose. The captain headed deep into the dark water and all the way down to the bottom. The seabed had turned to stone, but that didn't stop the captain. He hit the stone bottom so hard that the whole planet shook, and the stone turned to dust. He continued down through lava and fire, all the way to the bottom of the darkness. Climbing into the cold boat, he found a curled up Bubbly behind a steel door.

He sat down with Bubbly and gently said:

"I know you don't want to go to my new country, and I understand that. I also know that you don't want to be here. Everyone else is gathered for a party. I left them all because I don't want a party unless I know you're ok. Therefore, I want to give you an option that you didn't think existed. You can get out of here without having to come to the new country. I can build you a boat of your own. Would you like that? You can decide what it's going to look like and you're going to be the captain of it. The whole sea will be open to you, and you can go wherever you want."

Now Bubbly sat up: "Do you mean that?" The thought was mind-blowing. Captain of his own boat, with the vast sea open to him.

"But why? Why would you give me all that? You know I'm the one who sank this boat, right?"

"Bubbly, my Bubbly," the captain replied. "I held you in my hand long before you even came to life. I've seen you. I longed for you every day when you stood on your beach and every day when you were on my boat. I prepared a place for you in the new country and a seat at the party. I would do anything for you."

"I know things have been hard for you," he continued. "Giving you your own boat is my way of saying sorry. And I want you to know that if you ever want to dock your boat in my harbor, I'm going to throw you a big party."

Bubbly was so excited about this unexpected turnaround. Imagine becoming captain of a boat! He stood up and said:

"Let's go, this boat has seen better days."

The captain smiled, took him in his arms, and began the long journey back up. Bubbly tried to think about his new boat as they went up, but it was complicated: a strange feeling got in the way.

There in the captain's warm arms, he thought of everything he had been told. And how the captain had left everyone else behind just for him. The hatred that had been so strong in Bubbly vanished and gave way to a different feeling. He started crying and couldn't stop, he cried, and he cried. When they finally got up on land, the captain tried to put him down on the ground. But Bubbly clung to the captain's fur.

"Don't let me go," he whispered throuough the tears. "Please, don't let me go."

"But why?" the captain asked.

"Please, I want to stay, I don't want my own boat, I want to stay with you."

The captain was so glad he barely knew what to do. He held Bubbly in front of him so that he could look him in the eyes as he said:

"Yes, yes and a thousand yeses. I've longed to be with you all your life!"

With Bubbly in his arms, he ran back between the tables up to the stage shouting out:

"Bubbly is back, my child wants to stay, finally the party can begin!"

Everyone cheered and applauded, and the captain continued with a loud voice: "I want you all to know that I have longed for this day, to be here with you all. Wherever you've been, I've always seen you and have longed for you every day. I know some of you have had a pretty rough time. From now on, we're going to be together. Your name is written on the little sign in front of you because you're expected and wanted. For each of you, there is room prepared in this wonderful country. A long time ago, this place was a desert. Thanks to the Bucket Bearers watering, the ground is now covered with wonderful flowers."

The captain smiled at Bucky, who sat on the front row next to his mother. "Thank you very much for all you've done to make this country beautiful. Your lives will no longer be limited to ten days but will continue as for the rest of us. The captain's gaze continued to the tables where Mini-Goff and Pink sat.

"Goffs! My dear Goffs, you've done a wonderful job of preparing a whole world of rooms underground. There is a room for everyone with your name on the door, and there are cinemas, an adventure land, pools and everything we could wish for. Mini-Goff and Pink, a special thanks to you for helping the Goffs make peace."

The captain continued: "A bouncy city has landed here and anyone who likes to bounce is welcome to play there. Jackie and Boo will show you around."

As the captain spoke, someone had left their seat and come to the front. It was Snorkel. He was nervous as he looked up at Bubbly and said:

"Bubbly, can you forgive me? I should have done more to help you. Your seat is right next to mine. Do you want to come and sit there?"

Bubbly hurried down from the captain's arms. "I'm the one who should say sorry," he said. They took each other's hands and walked down to their seats.

The captain followed their steps with a big smile. Before they had reached their seats, he shouted: "Bubbly, this party needs bubbles, can you make some?"

While the band began to play Bubbly lifted his trunk and shot out hundreds of large, beautiful bubbles. The yellow butterflies tried to dive into the bubbles and everyone cheered. The captain looked at all the chaos with a big smile. He whispered to himself:

"I've longed for this moment for a thousand years. Finally all of my children are here with me."

Did you enjoy the world of purple skies?

The journey doesn't have to end here. Who else would like to here these stories? Maybe read them in a small group. Or why not just send a copy to a friend.

Hope to see you again soon...

Made in the USA
Coppell, TX
07 May 2024

32080009R20056